Four and Twenty Blackberries

Baked in Jadon's Pie

By Carol Van Zanden

popstradamus.com
Book design by Britt Sekulić
ISBN: 979-8-9916273-0-6

©2024 Copyright Carol Van Zanden. All rights reserved.
MADE IN USA

Part 1
Jadon Picks Blackberries

This is how to pick blackberries, Jadon.

Larkin wants to help pick blackberries, Grampa.

Here is another one, Larkin.

Jadon, are you going to pick blackberries for a pie or feed them to Larkin?

(Grandma washed the blackberries and made the crust.)

Part 2
Jadon Makes Blackberry Pie

First, I put the sugared blackberries in the pie crust.

Next, I put butter on the blackberries.

Butter!

More butter!

Then Grandma put the top crust on and I cut slits in the pie for the steam to come out.

The oven is getting hot.

Is the pie ready to go in the oven?

Yes!

It sure smells good!

Can we eat it, now?

Did you wonder why Jadon was wearing binoculars to make a blackberry pie?

He is a birdwatcher!

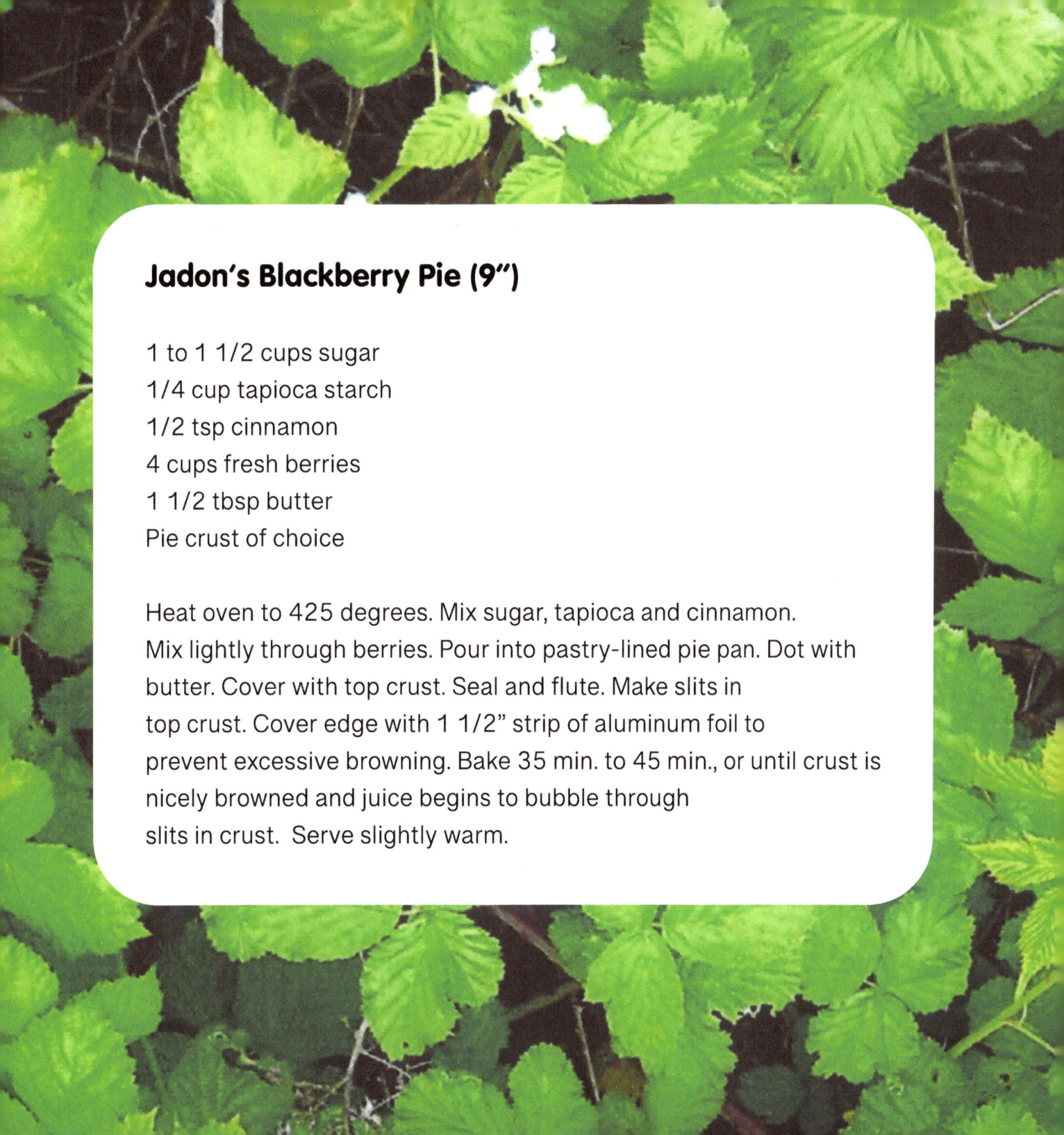

Jadon's Blackberry Pie (9")

1 to 1 1/2 cups sugar
1/4 cup tapioca starch
1/2 tsp cinnamon
4 cups fresh berries
1 1/2 tbsp butter
Pie crust of choice

Heat oven to 425 degrees. Mix sugar, tapioca and cinnamon. Mix lightly through berries. Pour into pastry-lined pie pan. Dot with butter. Cover with top crust. Seal and flute. Make slits in top crust. Cover edge with 1 1/2" strip of aluminum foil to prevent excessive browning. Bake 35 min. to 45 min., or until crust is nicely browned and juice begins to bubble through slits in crust. Serve slightly warm.

Special Thanks

Jadon, Grampa Ted, Larkin and Britt Sekulić

About the Author

Carol Van Zanden is a retired Home Economics and kindergarten teacher who has lived in the Pacific Northwest all her life. With her BA and MA in Education, her professional career spanned over 38 years in early elementary, high school and as a college and adult educator. She and her husband, Ted, raised their children in Oak Harbor, Washington.

Through the years, Carol combined her love of family and photography, capturing memories of their grandchildren's visits with her camera. Years ago, she cut and pasted a series of books together using photos of her granddaughter and grandson to be read to by their parents and written in early childhood language for them to read by themselves. Not knowing that someday her prayers would be answered, with the help of self-publishing, and collaborating with a local bookmaker, the books would be brought to life professionally for other parents to read to their children and for them to read themselves.

Did you enjoy this book? Try another book in the series:

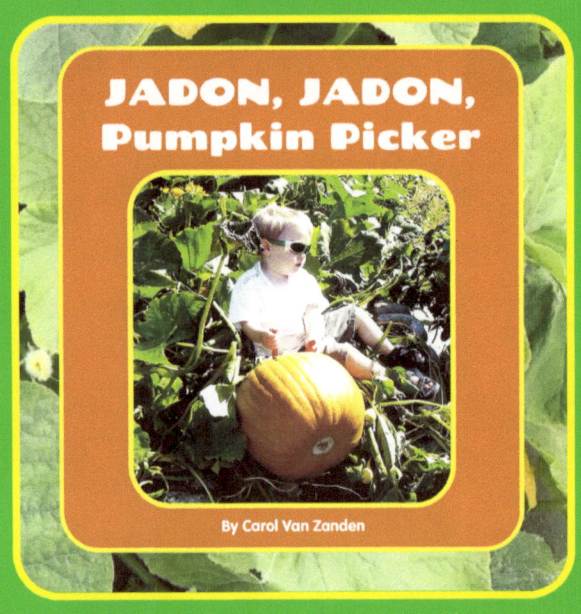